GREAT QUOTES

FROM

GREAT WOMEN

§ sourcebooks

Copyright © 2023 by Sourcebooks
Cover and internal design © 2023 by Sourcebooks
Cover design by Michelle Mayhall/Sourcebooks
Cover and internal images © (Maya Angelou) Michael Ochs Archives/Stringer/ Getty Images; (Ruth Bader Ginsburg) Steve Petteway, Collection of the Supreme Court of the United States, public domain; (Jane Goodall) Nick Stepowyj, CC BY-SA 2.0 via Wikimedia Commons; (Helen Keller) Library of Congress, Prints & Photographs Division, [LC-USZ62-11251], public domain; (Loretta Lynch) Chip Somodevilla/Staff/Getty Images; (Mother Teresa) Hulton Deutsch/Contributor/ Getty Images; (Michelle Obama) Paul Morigi/Stringer/Getty Images; (Rosa Parks) public domain; (Wilma Rudolph) Bettmann/Contributor/Getty Images; (Harriet Tubman) H. B. Lindsley, [LC-USZ62-7816], public domain; (Oprah Winfrey) Jaguar PS/Shutterstock, Inc.; (Malala Yousafzai) DFID - UK Department for International Development, CC BY-SA 2.0 via Wikimedia Commons; Thinkstock
Internal design by Danielle McNaughton/Sourcebooks

Published by Sourcebooks
P.O. Box 4410, Naperville, Illinois 60567-4410
(630) 961-3900
sourcebooks.com

Printed and bound in the United States of America.
VP 10 9 8 7 6 5 4 3 2 1

THIS JOURNAL BELONGS TO

You may not always have a comfortable life, and you will not always be able to solve all of the world's problems at once, but don't ever underestimate the importance you can have, because history has shown us that courage can be contagious and hope can take on a life of its own.

—MICHELLE OBAMA

INTRODUCTION

History's best-known women are an uplifting source of inspiration, comfort, and motivation for anyone looking to make their mark on the world. The quotes in this book come from artists, diplomats, activists, and leaders of all kinds.

No matter their source, the words collected throughout this journal reflect the resilience, compassion, and integrity of the women who said them. As you use this journal to plan, reflect, and create, we hope these words will guide you to live with intention and follow in the footsteps of these remarkable women.

Please enjoy the wisdom in this journal, and take inspiration from these tenacious, inventive, and pioneering women.

> I have sometimes been wildly despairing, acutely miserable, racked with sorrow, but through it all I still know quite certainly that just to be alive is a grand thing.
>
> —AGATHA CHRISTIE

Self-knowledge is no guarantee of happiness, but it is on the side of happiness and can supply the courage to fight for it.

—SIMONE DE BEAUVOIR

The essence of America—that which really unites us—is not ethnicity or nationality or religion. It is an idea—and what an idea it is: that you can come from humble circumstances and do great things.

—CONDOLEEZZA RICE

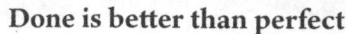

Done is better than perfect.

—SHERYL SANDBERG

Be gentle to all and stern with yourself.

—SAINT TERESA OF ÁVILA

Courage is the ladder on which all the other virtues mount.

—CLARE BOOTHE LUCE

Freedom does not mean being free of something,
but to be free to do something.

—ANGELA MERKEL

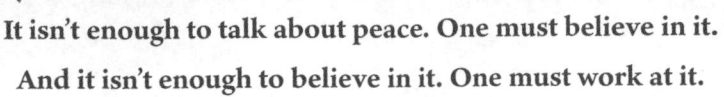

It isn't enough to talk about peace. One must believe in it.
And it isn't enough to believe in it. One must work at it.

—ELEANOR ROOSEVELT

The important thing is not what they think of me,
but what I think of them.

—QUEEN VICTORIA

Success is terrifying.

Like happiness, it is often appreciated in retrospect.

—JULIE ANDREWS

I like to praise and reward loudly, to blame quietly.

—CATHERINE THE GREAT

Love is a fruit in season at all times,

and within reach of every hand.

—MOTHER TERESA

A mistake in judgment isn't fatal,
but too much anxiety about judgment is.

—PAULINE KAEL

> **Yesterday I dared to struggle. Today I dare to win.**
>
> —BERNADETTE DEVLIN

Humility is no substitute for a good personality.

—FRAN LEBOWITZ

> Mistakes are a fact of life.
>
> It is the response to the error that counts.
>
> —NIKKI GIOVANNI

> Once I had asked God for one or two extra inches in height,
> but instead he made me as tall as the sky, so high that
> I could not measure myself... By giving me this height to
> reach people, he has also given me great responsibilities.
>
> —MALALA YOUSAFZAI

Be passionate. Be courageous. Be your best.

—GABRIELLE GIFFORDS

Science progresses best when observations
force us to alter our preconceptions.

—VERA RUBIN

You cannot, you cannot use someone else's fire. You can only use your own. And in order to do that, you must first be willing to believe that you have it.

—AUDRE LORDE

Sometimes we just simply have to find a way. The moment we decide to fulfill something, we can do anything.

—GRETA THUNBERG

The most effective way to do it is to do it.

—AMELIA EARHART

Life isn't a matter of milestones, but of moments.

—ROSE KENNEDY

A surplus of effort could overcome a deficit of confidence.

—SONIA SOTOMAYOR

One's philosophy is not best expressed in words;
it is expressed in the choices one makes.

—ELEANOR ROOSEVELT

**If you worry about who is going to get credit,
you don't get much work done.**

—DOROTHY HEIGHT

Fearlessness is like a muscle. I know from my own life that the more I exercise it the more natural it becomes to not let my fears run me.

—ARIANNA HUFFINGTON

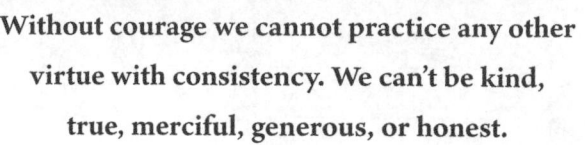

Without courage we cannot practice any other
virtue with consistency. We can't be kind,
true, merciful, generous, or honest.

—MAYA ANGELOU

When you have a good idea and you've tried it and you
know it's going to work, go ahead and do it, because it is
much easier to apologize later than it is to get permission.

—GRACE HOPPER

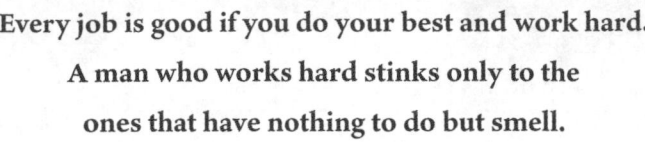

Every job is good if you do your best and work hard.
A man who works hard stinks only to the
ones that have nothing to do but smell.

—LAURA INGALLS WILDER

> The day will come when man will recognize woman as his peer, not only at the fireside, but in councils of the nation. Then, and not until then, will there be the perfect comradeship, the ideal union between the sexes that shall result in the highest development of the race.

—SUSAN B. ANTHONY

One child, one teacher, one pen, and one
book can change the world.

—MALALA YOUSAFZAI

I am not going to die, I'm going home like a shooting star.

—SOJOURNER TRUTH

Be ahead of your time—that's what you have to do.

—BILLIE JEAN KING

> **When people made up their minds that they wanted to be free and took action, then there was change.**
>
> —ROSA PARKS

A lot of people notice when you succeed, but
they don't see what it takes to get there.

—DAWN STALEY

Don't confuse having a career with having a life. They are not the same.

—HILLARY CLINTON

People cannot change their habits without
first changing their way of thinking.

—MARIE KONDO

Art is a guaranty of sanity.

—LOUISE BOURGEOIS

Somewhere behind the athlete you've become and the hours of practice and the coaches who have pushed you is a little girl who fell in love with the game and never looked back... Play for her.

—MIA HAMM

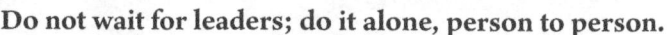

Do not wait for leaders; do it alone, person to person.

—MOTHER TERESA

For there are no new ideas.
There are only new ways of making them felt.

—AUDRE LORDE

I'd rather regret the things I've done
than regret the things I haven't done.

—LUCILLE BALL

We are not put on this earth to accumulate victories and trophies and avoid failures, but rather to be whittled and sandpapered down until what's left is who we truly are.

—ARIANNA HUFFINGTON

> The real wealth of the nation lies in the resources of the earth—soil, water, forests, minerals, and wildlife.
>
> —RACHEL CARSON

I don't go by a rule book,
because I lead from the heart, not the head.

—DIANA, PRINCESS OF WALES

Love recognizes no barriers. It jumps hurdles, leaps fences, penetrates walls to arrive at its destination full of hope.

—MAYA ANGELOU

Intense love does not measure, it just gives.

—MOTHER TERESA

I had reasoned this out in my mind; there was one of two things I had a right to, liberty, or death; if I could not have one, I would have the other; for no man should take me alive; I should fight for my liberty as long as my strength lasted, and when the time came for me to go, the Lord would let them take me.

—HARRIET TUBMAN

_____

You must learn to be still in the midst of activity
and to be vibrantly alive in repose.

—INDIRA GANDHI

Happiness cannot come from without.
It must come from within.

—HELEN KELLER

Be less curious about people and more curious about ideas.

—MARIE CURIE

You can't use up creativity.
The more you use, the more you have.

—MAYA ANGELOU

If you learn something new every day, you
can teach something new every day.

—MARTHA STEWART

A lot of people are waiting for Martin Luther King or Mahatma Gandhi to come back—but they are gone. We are it. It is up to us. It is up to you.

—MARIAN WRIGHT EDELMAN

Every generation has to fight anew the battle for liberty.

—MARGARET THATCHER

No one can arrive from being talented alone.
God gives talent; work transforms talent into genius.

—ANNA PAVLOVA

I think knowing what you cannot do is more important than knowing what you can do. In fact, that's good taste.

—LUCILLE BALL

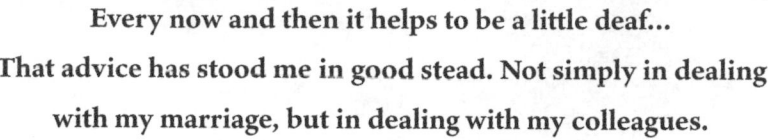

Every now and then it helps to be a little deaf...
That advice has stood me in good stead. Not simply in dealing
with my marriage, but in dealing with my colleagues.

—RUTH BADER GINSBURG

If you concentrate on what you have, you will always end up having more... If you focus on what you don't have, you will never, ever, ever have enough.

—OPRAH WINFREY

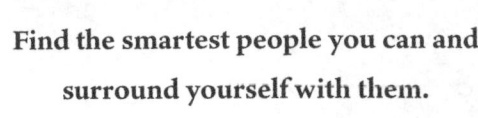

Find the smartest people you can and surround yourself with them.

—MARISSA MAYER

The right way is not always the popular and easy way.
Standing for right when it is unpopular
is a true test of moral character.

—MARGARET CHASE SMITH

You have only one chance to raise your child.

—JACQUELINE KENNEDY ONASSIS

Do not live someone else's life and someone else's idea of what womanhood is. Womanhood is you. Womanhood is everything that's inside of you.

—VIOLA DAVIS

> Use your life to serve the world, and you
> will find that it also serves you.
>
> —OPRAH WINFREY

The one important thing I have learnt over the years is the difference between taking one's work seriously and taking oneself seriously. The first is imperative and the second disastrous.

—MARGOT FONTEYN

Success doesn't change you; fame does.

—WHITNEY HOUSTON

My spirit is as strong as ever. I'm still fighting to
make the world a better place, and you can, too.

—GABRIELLE GIFFORDS

What we have once enjoyed we can never lose.
All that we love deeply becomes a part of us.

—HELEN KELLER

The most difficult thing is the decision to
act. The rest is merely tenacity.

—AMELIA EARHART

The task of the educator of young children lies in seeing that the child does not confound good with immobility and evil with activity.

—MARIA MONTESSORI

When people show you who they are, believe them.

—MAYA ANGELOU

Success is only meaningful and enjoyable

if it feels like your own.

—MICHELLE OBAMA

The courage to be vulnerable is not about winning or losing, it's about the courage to show up when you can't predict or control the outcome.

—BRENÉ BROWN

It is not easy to find happiness in ourselves,
and it is not possible to find it elsewhere.

—AGNES REPPLIER

Careers are a jungle gym, not a ladder.

—PATTIE SELLERS

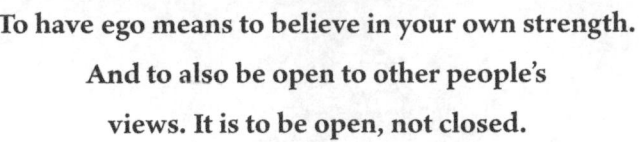

To have ego means to believe in your own strength. And to also be open to other people's views. It is to be open, not closed.

—BARBRA STREISAND

Without leaps of imagination, or dreaming,
we lose the excitement of possibilities.
Dreaming, after all, is a form of planning.

—GLORIA STEINEM

> **If your actions create a legacy that inspires others to dream more, learn more, do more, and become more, then you are an excellent leader.**
>
> —DOLLY PARTON

Whatever you want in life, other people are going to want it too. Believe in yourself enough to accept the idea that you have an equal right to it.

—DIANE SAWYER

> When we are listened to, it creates us, makes us unfold and expand. Ideas actually begin to grow within us and come to life.
>
> —BRENDA UELAND

**I don't even know who someone is until
I've seen how they handle adversity.**

—SHONDA RHIMES

> **It took me quite a long time to develop a voice,**
> **and now that I have it, I am not going to be silent.**
>
> —MADELEINE ALBRIGHT

If your dreams do not scare you, they are not big enough.

—ELLEN JOHNSON SIRLEAF

Whatever can happen to anyone can happen to me.

—MURIEL RUKEYSER

I never dreamed about success. I worked for it.

—ESTÉE LAUDER

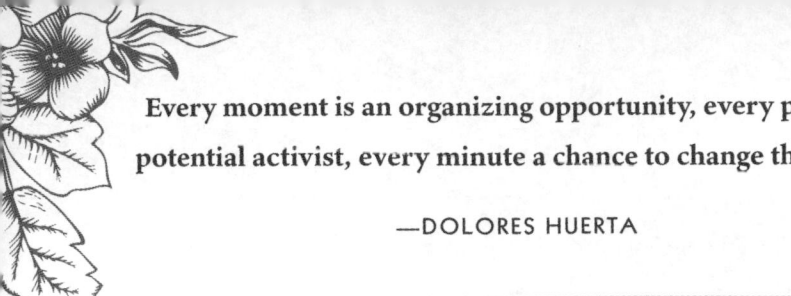

Every moment is an organizing opportunity, every person a potential activist, every minute a chance to change the world.

—DOLORES HUERTA

If you don't see a clear path for what you want,
sometimes you have to make it yourself.

—MINDY KALING

> **Our life is our business and if you don't treat your life like a business, you're going to go out of business.**
>
> —TABITHA BROWN

I'll tell you what freedom is to me. No fear.

—NINA SIMONE

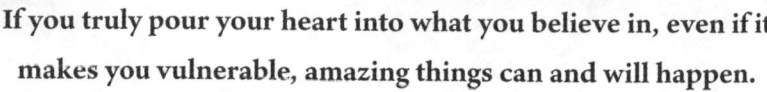

If you truly pour your heart into what you believe in, even if it makes you vulnerable, amazing things can and will happen.

—EMMA WATSON